Virginia Born

Amazing People from the Commonwealth
By David Messick
Illustrated by Liu Light

Virginia Born
Amazing People from the Commonwealth

By David Messick
Original Illustrations by Lucia Liu
Puppet Images Rainbow Productions, Inc.

Puppets created by Laura Baldwin and Jill Harrington

Rainbow puppeteers include James Cooper, Wesley Huff, Alyssa Jones, and David & Joshua Messick

Design and layout by Virginia Gabriele

ISBN: 978-1-7332484-8-8
First printing / Printed in the USA
Rainbow Puppet Publications
18 Easthill Court, Hampton, Virginia 23664
Rainbow Puppet Productions is a non-profit, educational entertainment company

Thanks to
Traci Massie, Curtis Johnson, Erin Matteson, and Optima Health
Laura Baldwin, Tony Gabriele, Jim & Linda Haas and the
Academy of Dance and Gymnastics, Jerry Hansbrough,
David & Stephanie Messick, Marcy Messick, Richard Moyer, Jr.,
The Searchers Group, Nancy Kent Swilley, and Rose West.

In Memory of
Mrs. Barham and Mrs. Campbell...
Two teachers who made a huge difference to me.

"Start where you are.

Use what you have.

Do what you can."

Arthur Ashe

Contents

Introduction

I was born in the Commonwealth of Virginia, and I have great love for my home state. The scenery is beautiful and diverse. In a single day, you can watch the sunrise over the Atlantic Ocean and just a few hours later, kayak on our crystal-clear lakes. You can explore our cool, underground caverns, and then watch the sun set over our snow-capped mountains.

It's not just the diversity of climate and natural wonders that make Virginia special, it's also the diversity of people and their experiences that enrich the state. We have been blessed to have many wonderful people born here. So, let's meet some of the amazing people who were Virginia born.

Sunrise on the Chesapeake Bay. *(Author)*

Pocahontas
Our First Ambassador

Pocahontas had no trouble spotting the deer tracks by the side of the river.

"They're right here. I knew I'd find them," she said as her toes sunk into the cool mud. "How did my brothers miss them?"

Her father smiled. At only seven years old, she had the skills to track animals as well as any of her brothers and she could spot ripe berries before her sisters. In her mind she could out-run and out-track any of her siblings. She was Powhatan's favorite daughter... and he had many daughters.

As *Paramount Chief*, Powhatan's reach and influence were great -- stretching from the Eastern Shore of Virginia to eastern North Carolina. As many as 32 chiefs and leaders answered to him and he was a stern taskmaster. He had to be. Survival depended on knowing the land, the plants, the waters, and the creatures. There was a time to fish, a time to hunt, a time to plant, and a time to harvest. A little laziness or miscalculation could mean a winter without food.

Powhatan climbed up the small dune of sand, looked out to the bay and then to the forest behind. He called his daughter, who quickly ran to him.

"Look Pocahontas, look all around, as far as your eyes can see," he said. "Our people have been blessed."

"Streams and springs provide water to drink. The sea provides fish and oysters. The land provides berries and the soil allows us to plant corn. There are animals all around to provide us with fur for warmth and meat to eat. The sky provides rain for our plants and a wide space for the birds to fly."

Pocahontas looked up to her father and smiled.

Placing his hand on her

Indian Princess

POCAHONTAS

1595 - 1616

of

Werowocomoco

Wicomico

Statue at her birthplace, in Gloucester in the eastern part of Virginia. *(Author)*

8

shoulder, Powhatan kneeled down beside his daughter as he looked out across the sea. "Who could ever dream of a land like ours... a land of such riches?"

How could Powhatan have known that over 3,000 miles away, on the other side of the Atlantic Ocean, there were people dreaming of just those riches?

Starting in England on December 19, 1606, Captain Christopher Newport led a group of 144 men and boys in three ships: the Godspeed, the Discovery, and the Susan Constant. Almost five months later, after a dangerous voyage, Christopher Newport found what he was looking for. On May 13, 1607, they arrived in Virginia and built a triangular wooden fortress. They started a *colony* that they called Jamestown. They named it in honor of their King James. This is the same King James who authorized the noted English translation of the Bible.

The settlers had picked a swampy, mosquito-infested spot for their fort. The water was muddy and barely drinkable. They were not prepared for life at Jamestown and often needed to get help from the local tribes. Sometimes, the settlers and tribes got along. At other times, they did not.

Pocahontas enjoyed visiting the settlers and playing

with their children. When she could, she would also bring them corn and other food.

Captain John Smith, one of the early settlers, wrote that he was once captured by members of Powhatan's tribe and threatened with death. According to his story, Pocahontas burst onto the scene and successfully pleaded for his life. Historians are not sure if this really happened or if the story was *exaggerated*.

Decorative plate, from the Jamestown 350th Commemoration. Courtesy of the Pocahontas Museum in Gloucester, VA. *(Author)*

What is certain is that when times got especially bad for the *colonist*s, they conspired with a neighboring tribe to kidnap Pocahontas. It was the hope of the English that they would be able to trade Powhatan's favorite daughter for food and supplies.

During this time, Pocahontas was on her own. Separated from her father and family, she may also have felt abandoned by Captain John Smith who perhaps could have rescued her.

She took matters into her own hands. She learned to read. She studied the Bible and converted to Christianity. She would be the bridge between the English and her people.

John Rolfe, one of the settlers, fell in love with Pocahontas. As a planter, perhaps he appreciated her understanding of the balance of nature. The two were married with the blessing of both Powhatan and the Virginia Governor Thomas Dale. He called the marriage a "knot to bind the peace." This Pocahontas Peace would last for the next eight years.

THE BAPTISM OF POCAHONTAS·VIRGINIA

Native American students at Hampton University helped pay for this stained-glass window inside St. John's Episcopal church in Hampton. It shows the baptism of Pocahontas. *(Author)*

John and Pocahontas had a child and went to England where she was a sensation. Most people were thrilled to see Pocahontas as she visited London, which was the capital of the *British* Empire. She was puzzled to hear some whisper and call her and her people savages. Pocahontas probably had the same feeling for the people in London and the way they lived. Almost all of the trees were gone. A thick cloud of smoke hung over the city. When the wind blew in a certain direction, a foul smell blew in from the polluted Thames River. It was common for people to throw their waste out of their windows into the public streets.

Pocahontas became an ambassador for her people. She worked to create good feelings, peace, and understanding with others. She shared her thoughts about respecting the environment and one another.

Pocahontas never returned to Virginia. She contracted a breathing condition and died outside of London. Over 400 years later, through books, films, children's toys, and costumes, she is remembered around the world. Her work as an ambassador continues as she reminds us to respect others and protect our natural resources.

This statue can be found at her burial place in Gravesend, England. *(Claudine Van Massenhove / Shutterstock)*

Lake Matoaka on the campus of The College of William and Mary is named after Pocahontas. *(Author)*

A New World?

Christopher Newport, John Smith, and many others referred to North America as a "New World." But it wasn't a new world. It was only new to them. The term "New World" would have, at the very least, been confusing to the inhabitants that they met. It fails to recognize the people who were here long before Europe set out on its exploration of the Americas.

One Lady... Four Names

While she is best known today as Pocahontas, that was one of four names she was called during her short life. Her name at birth was Amonute but her close family called her Matoaka. Her nickname, Pocahontas, meant "mischief maker" or "playful one." Finally, when she was baptized and married, she became known to the English as Rebecca.

Pearl Bailey recording "Big Mamma." *(Everett Collection)*

Another Virginia Ambassador

Actress and singer Pearl Bailey was born in Newport News in eastern Virginia. Pearl won a *Tony Award* for starring in the long running Broadway musical "Hello, Dolly!" She is perhaps best known today as the voice of "Big Mamma" in the Walt Disney classic "The Fox and the Hound."

She was such a beloved entertainer that President Lyndon B. Johnson named her the United Nations Ambassador of Love. Her job was to build good will with nations around the world.

There is a public library in downtown Newport News named in her honor.

Ella Fitzgerald
The Queen of Jazz

Even today, industrial downtown Newport News would seem an unlikely location for the birth of a queen. There is the shipping terminal with trucks waiting to be loaded. There are many train lines with coal cars waiting to be unloaded. There are the mountains of coal being gently sprayed with water to keep down the dust. Then, of course, there is the largest shipyard in the country, building huge nuclear-powered submarines and ships.

In 1917, it would seem even more unlikely that a girl born in Newport News would one day be proclaimed the "Queen of Jazz." Just as the giant shipyard would create ships that would connect America with the rest of the world, one day she would use her musical talents to connect with the entire world. But those days were a long way off...

The loud whistle at the shipyard has awakened little Ella Fitzgerald from her sleep. She's alone in her dark room. At first, she's scared to be all alone. Then she remembers what her mother would say as she would leave for work as a maid, "You're never really alone, Ella. There's music all around to keep you company. You just have to listen for it." And Ella has a good ear.

Downstairs, her father is strumming chords on his guitar. "Strum…. Strum." The coal trains are starting their slow trek up town and on to Richmond.

Ella was honored by the U.S. Post Office.

The metal wheels clunk on the uneven tracks, "Ca-chunk… Ca-chunk." Occasionally, the trolley bell would ring as it made stops, taking workers home. "Clang, Clang… Clang, Clang." And in the distance, there were deep whistles from a tug boat. "Wooo!"

These random sounds somehow, almost magically start to blend in little Ella's head and become their own symphony of sounds, "Strum, strum, ca-chunk… Strum,

strum, ca-chunk… Clang, Clang, Clang, Clang… Wooo!"
Soon, she is comforted back to sleep.

Ella and her mother left Newport News while she was very young. They moved to New York where she excelled in school and in the music of her church. All of this would change when her mother died from injuries in a car accident.

Ella was now adrift, missing school, making bad choices and associating with a dangerous crowd. Again, she felt all alone, like that night in her room. Once again, music would come to her rescue.

Ella entered a talent contest at the legendary Apollo Theater in Harlem, New York. It was her intent to perform a dance as her talent but after seeing the other dance act, she changed her mind. Instead, she sang. Thanks to her clear, beautiful voice, she won!

Ella's singing was unique. She studied the top radio stars of the day but then added her own qualities. She would often sing the first verse and chorus flawlessly and as written. Here, she demonstrated her appreciation of the songwriters' words and music. Then, like a jazz trumpet player, she would "*scat*" or improvise rhythmic sounds that fell perfectly into the band's arrangement. It was like the sounds she had made in her room when she was a little girl.

Her "scatting" became her trademark and those who knew her noticed that she would often pick up on sounds she had heard throughout the day and add them into her performance. It was just like her mother had told her long ago, "there's music all around."

Her recordings and personal appearances brought her international acclaim. She was given the title "First Lady of Song" and "The Queen of Jazz."

Ella being recognized at the Hampton Jazz Festival. *(Kenneth Silver / Daily Press)*

The Ella Fitzgerald Theater in Newport News hosts international stars and offers opportunities for up-and-coming artists in the community. *(Author)*

In 1979, Ella returned to Virginia to perform at the Hampton Jazz Festival's "Tribute to Ella Fitzgerald." The mayors of both Newport News and Hampton came onstage to recognize her.

Thousands of fans stood and cheered their returning star. Perhaps she even closed her eyes and thought about her mother. She had been right. Because of her music, Ella Fitzgerald was not alone.

Newport News continues to celebrate the "Queen of Jazz" with this sign across from her theater. *(Author)*

Other Virginia Singers

(agwilson / Shutterstock)

Pharrell Williams (Virginia Beach) Pharrell has made many people "Happy" with his song of the same name and his many efforts to help others. He has 13 *Grammy Awards*.

(Nikola Spasenoski / Shutterstock)

Missy Elliott (Portsmouth) She's been called the "Queen of Rap" and has been awarded four *Grammy Awards*. Like Pharrell, she has performed at the Super Bowl.

Bruce Hornsby (Williamsburg) An amazing musician on piano and other instruments, Bruce has found success combining many musical styles including Rock, Country, Bluegrass, Classical and Jazz. Along the way, he has won three *Grammy Awards*.

(Wiki Commons)

This car, once owned by Wayne Newton, is one of many treasures on display at the Virginia Musical Museum in Williamsburg. *(Author)*

Wayne Newton (Norfolk) Known as Mr. Las Vegas, Wayne Newton is a gifted entertainer. He sings, he plays 13 instruments, and he's been performing in Las Vegas since 1959.

Wayne has appeared in a James Bond movie, competed on "Dancing with the Stars," and serves as the Chairman of the USO Celebrity Circle. In his "spare

(Depart. of Defense / TSGT David J Ahlschwede)

time" he became an award-winning Arabian horse breeder. His love of horses came from his time on his uncle's farm in Virginia.

George Washington
The Man Who Would *NOT* Be King

Virginia has been called "The Mother of Presidents." Eight U.S. Presidents were born in the state. There are great stories that could be told about any one of them but it was the actions of the first that allowed our country to be born. George Washington was so popular that he could have set himself up as permanent President or "King" of the new nation. He was wise enough to choose a different way.

George was born in Popes Creek, in eastern Virginia

A 1930's re-creation of George Washington's first home in Westmoreland County, VA. *(Author)*

on February 22, 1732. Growing up, George was athletic. He loved horses and the outdoors. He enjoyed math but struggled with writing.

When George's beloved step-brother Lawrence died, a position opened in the militia. George answered the call and took over his brother's position as a military officer. George distinguished himself during the French and Indian War. He then returned to his home, Mount Vernon, where he married and ran his huge farm.

During this time, Virginia and the other colonies were becoming more and more frustrated with *Britain*. They were being taxed to pay for Britain's war against France. A tax on tea was the final straw. In protest, colonists threw cases of tea into the Boston, Massachusetts harbor.

The colonies felt they were being taxed without a say in their government. They were willing to go to war to win their independence from England and they called on George Washington to lead them. George answered the call.

It was a long and difficult war, lasting over eight years. The colonies' soldiers were frequently underfed, undersupplied, and unpaid. But, they trusted and

George Washington's beloved home, Mount Vernon. *(Author)*

respected Washington. Unlike his British opponents, Washington would favor frequent smaller raids over large scale battles. The colonists would hide in trees and beside roadways wearing clothes that blended in with the surroundings. The British would fight in the open, wearing easy to see red uniforms, hence their nickname, "The Redcoats." As you can imagine, the British were easy targets.

In the end, the colonists outlasted the British and victory was won on a battlefield in Yorktown, Virginia. George Washington had won the Revolutionary War. But, unlike most people who win wars, George did not want any more power for himself. He just wanted to return to his beloved home, Mount Vernon.

Even King George III of England took notice. When told that Washington would walk away from all the power he could have had, the king said, "If he does that, he will be the greatest man on earth."

His return to Mount Vernon was short-lived. When the United States needed a leader, a President, there was one man who was trusted and admired above all others. Once again, George Washington answered the call.

Washington made it clear right away that he was not a king. He refused to be addressed with phrases like "Your majesty" or "Your highness." Instead, he was to be addressed as "Mr. President."

As President, he was now responsible for the budget of the growing nation. And he was the Commander in Chief, responsible for the military and the defense of the country, and he would appoint judges for the Supreme Court.

After serving four years in the job, George Washington was elected to a second term but that was it. When asked to serve a third term, he answered the call in an unusual way. He said, "no."

George felt that if he continued as President it would be no different from having a king. And so, the amazing happened. A new President was elected and power peacefully transferred from one leader to another… without war… without violence.

A classic book illustration of the cherry tree myth. *(Shutterstock)*

Someone Told a Lie!

A children's story was created about young George chopping down his father's cherry tree with a hatchet. When asked about the tree, George supposedly told his father, "I can't tell a lie. I did cut it with my hatchet. It was me." Actually, this story was invented by a writer after George's death. It's a good lesson in honesty, even if the incident is not true.

Wooden Stones... Not Wooden Teeth

George Washington was troubled with bad teeth, which he lost one by one. Despite rumors, he did *not* have wooden teeth. His false teeth were made of carved ivory and human teeth set in lead. They were painful to wear.

Exterior of George Washington's Mount Vernon. Made of wood, not stone. *(Author)*

Even the fancy oak walls of his office aren't real. They are local pine wood painted to look like oak. *(Author)*

He did have wooden "stone walls" on his house. To make his home look impressive, the pine boards on the outside of Mount Vernon were cut to resemble carved stone. They were then covered with a sand and paint mixture. The process was very durable. Over 80% of the boards on the home today are from George Washington's time in the house.

Other Presidents Born in Virginia

Thomas Jefferson (Shadwell) 3rd President. He was the primary author of the Declaration of Independence and creator of the University of Virginia.

James Madison (Port Conway) 4th President. He is considered "Father of the Constitution."

James Monroe (Monroe Hall) 5th President. He made clear the U.S. would not tolerate interference from countries outside of our hemisphere.

William Henry Harrison (Charles City) 9th President. He gave the longest acceptance speech and had the shortest presidency of only 31 days.

John Tyler (Charles City) 10th President. When Harrison died, Tyler became the first Vice President to succeed to the presidency.

Zachary Taylor (Barboursville) 12th President. He was a war hero who died 16 months into his presidency.

Woodrow Wilson (Staunton) 28th President. He worked to create the League of Nations and the National Parks System.

Bill Robinson
The Mayor of Harlem

In Richmond, there is a small, triangle shaped park created where three busy streets come together. Crossing the street by foot or by car would be very confusing if it weren't for the traffic lights that safely direct walkers and drivers. At the center of this park is the statue of a man dancing on a flight of stairs. He is still considered by many to be the greatest tap dancer that ever lived. He is also the very generous man who paid for the original street lights that allowed children to cross the street safely. He spent most of his life sharing his gift of dance and sharing his earnings with others.

Luther Robinson was born in Richmond in 1878, twelve years and a day after the American Civil War ended. According to his friends, Luther hated his name and traded with his brother. It was also in Richmond that he picked up the nickname "Bojangles." That's how he became Bill "Bojangles" Robinson.

By the time he was six, both of his parents were dead and he and his brother were raised by his grandmother. She had been born a slave who was freed at the end of the war. By now, in poor health, she was ill-prepared to raise two boys.

Bill spent his youth downtown, picking up odd jobs like shining shoes and picking beans in the market. He'd also spend time outside the theaters of Richmond dancing in the streets to entertain people entering or leaving the theaters. When folks asked how he was doing he'd smile and use a phrase he made famous, "It's copasetic!" which meant "everything is just fine."

At home, everything was not "just fine." Bill's grandmother, a strict woman, set in her ways, could not tolerate the boys dancing in the street. "Don't come near this house if you've been dancing!" she had warned. Bill was finding success as a dancer and so he left, heading first to Washington, DC. After serving his country for a time during the

The Bill Robinson statue in Richmond. *(Author)*

Spanish-American War, Bill made his way to New York where he became a star.

A modern traffic signal by the Bill Robinson statue. *(Author)*

What made Bill's dancing unique is his flawless execution of every single step. He made everything look simple and effortless. Every step he made was perfect in sound, clarity, and presentation. Unlike many tap dancers, who use metal taps attached to their shoes, Bill's shoes had wooden taps. They were custom made in Chicago and the moment the taps became slightly worn, he would order a brand-new pair.

By the early 1930's, the most popular star during this time was a little girl named Shirley Temple. She would appear in one film after another as a child overcoming unbelievable hardships. No matter what she faced, she faced it with bravery and a smile. Her films gave hope to everyone who was hurting across the country. When Hollywood producers wanted to give her a dancing co-star, they turned to Bill Robinson.

In his first film with Shirley, Bill performed his staircase dance. It was a complicated number that he had taken years to perfect. The movie producers asked him to add to the number by having Shirley join him at the end. Bill knew it would be difficult for anyone, especially a little girl, but she did it. Her hard work impressed him and the two became lifelong friends. He even bought her a tiny car to drive around the studio!

Bill's four films with Shirley were slowly breaking

Bill Robinson and Shirley Temple perform the staircase dance. *(Public domain publicity photo)* down rules and barriers that existed in the film business. A black man holding hands and dancing with a white girl would have been forbidden had it not been for America's love of these two performers. In a later film, Bill became Shirley's guardian, fully responsible for her safety as they traveled across the country. These seemingly small steps were actually making a difference in the way people viewed one another across America.

Bill was now one of the most famous dancers in the movies. But his great fame was coupled with his great generosity. He always remembered his tough childhood and wherever he went, if Bill saw people in trouble, he would help. Now living in the Harlem section of New York, if he saw someone hungry, he gave them food. If he saw someone thrown out of their apartment, he'd pay their rent and hire workers to return the family to their home. In between two and three shows a day, he'd rush across town to perform for free at a benefit for whatever charity asked for his help. His big heart was so appreciated that Bill was named the "Mayor of Harlem."

A few weeks before he died, Bill offered advice to an up-and-coming dancer. "It's not what you do on the stage… it's what you do after you leave the stage."

Bill's final film was "Stormy Weather" with Lena Horne and Cab Calloway. He was happy to finally wear the sharp looking suits he loved to wear on stage and in public. *(Public Domain Publicity Photo)*

Bill Robinson left the stage on November 25, 1949. His funeral was the largest ever held in New York City. One person after another spoke of his great skill as a dancer. Finally, his minister stood up and said, "No one ever raised as much money for human suffering as Bill Robinson... Bill fed them when they were hungry. He danced for them to get clothes when they were naked. There wasn't any charity that he'd ever turn down... the greatest rule in life is to 'love they neighbors as thyself.'"

Bill "Bojangles" Robinson shared his love for others onstage and off.

Modern dance legend Savion Glover (left) performing onstage. He provided the tap dancing in the movie "Happy Feet" and appeared in a movie about Bill Robinson. *(lev radin / Shutterstock)*

Sammy Davis, Jr. (right) learned tap steps from Bill Robinson. He later sang "Mr. Bojangles" in his act. *(Nationaal Archief / Public Domain)*

Tap dancing is an American art form which blends the many cultures that came to the United States. African tribal dances combine with high stepping Irish jigs along with English clogging and Dutch wooden shoe dances.

Tell the Truth

The chicken restaurant "Bojangles'" was named after a popular song called "Mr. Bojangles." Despite popular belief, that song was not really about Bill Robinson. It was really about a New Orleans dancer who used the name.

(Bruce VanLoon / Shutterstock)

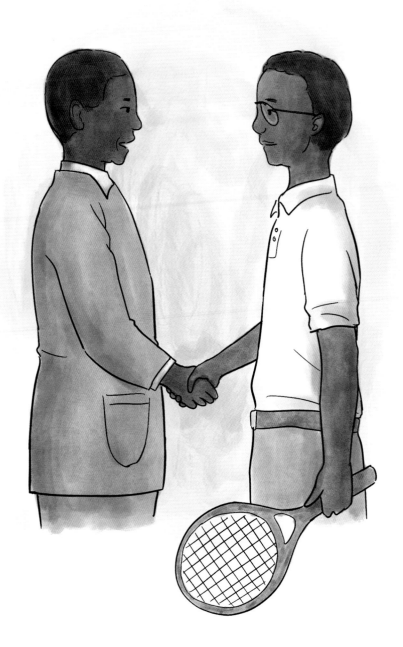

Arthur Ashe
A Hero *On* and Off the Court

Bill Bojangles is not the only Richmond-born hero honored with a statue. In the middle of a beautiful neighborhood in the city, you'll see a statue of a man holding a tennis racket in one hand and a book in the other. Children are jumping up, reaching for both the opportunities offered by sports and by a good education. This statue honors Arthur Ashe, a great tennis player who used his skills and influence to improve the lives of many around the world.

His accomplishments on the tennis court are legendary. He was the first, and only African American to be ranked number one in the world. He was the first African American to be selected for the U.S. Davis Cup team. He is the only black male tennis player to win both Wimbledon and the U.S. Open. He also won the Australian Open, the French Open, and the South African Open. Perhaps his win in the South African Open speaks most to the character and determination of Arthur Ashe.

Born in 1942, his mother died when he was only six years old. He was raised by his father. He soon

Arthur Ashe was honored by the U.S. Postal service with this stamp. *(Shutterstock)*

picked up tennis, which he could play at the black-only public park near his home. His skill caught the attention of others who encouraged and taught him along the way. These generous mentors helped Arthur excel at the sport, earning a scholarship at the University of California in Los Angeles.

It was while he was in college that his team was asked to play in a tournament at the Balboa Bay Club in Newport Beach, California. His team was invited. He was not. The club refused to let a black player participate. While his coach was willing to pull the entire team out of the event, Arthur encouraged them to remain and play. There would be a time to take action later.

He would get his chance to shine when he earned a spot to play at Wimbledon. Again, a generous person came forward to encourage Arthur and pay his expenses in order to play.

While he didn't win his first time at Wimbledon, he was constantly improving. He became the first African American

Arthur in action. *(Nationaal Archief Fotocollectie Anefo / Rob Bogaerts)*

to compete in the Davis Cup. What followed was an amazing career where his talent was on display all around the world. Well, almost all around the world.

Time and again, Arthur was denied entry to play in the South African Open. In the 1960's census, 68% of the people in South Africa were black. But there were laws which kept them from enjoying the rights and opportunities afforded to the white rulers of the country. In 1962, Nelson Mandela, a black lawyer and activist in South Africa had been imprisoned for trying to lead the majority of people to fairness.

Arthur agreed that things needed to change in South Africa. He used his influence as an international tennis star to help shine a spotlight on the problems in South

The U.S. Open is played at the Arthur Ashe Stadium in New York. It is the largest tennis stadium in the world. *(Shutterstock)*

Africa. Working with others, he got South Africa kicked out of the international Davis Cup. Finally, bowing to pressure, the South African government allowed Arthur to play in the South African Open.

He won the doubles match playing with a former white rival, Tom Okur. A black player and a white player, once opponents on the court, now showed that opponents could work together and win. And they did win doubles at the South African Open.

Arthur did not stop there. Working with entertainers like Bruce Springsteen, he continued to put pressure on the South African government to make changes. Finally, in 1989 a new president was elected and the laws which harmed black South Africans were later eliminated.

Nelson Mandela, still the symbolic leader of the majority in South Africa was released from prison in 1990. His first stop on a visit to New York City was to thank Arthur for his hard work. Then, in 1994, Nelson became the President of South Africa.   He brought healing and unity to the nation.

Arthur died at the young age of 42. He had contracted HIV while receiving care for a heart attack. At the time, there was great fear of people who had HIV. Arthur spent his last year helping educate people about the disease.

As an athlete, an educator, and an advocate, Arthur's presence is still felt in Richmond and around the world.

The Arthur Ashe statue in Richmond. *(Author)*

There have been so many great athletes from Virginia. Here are just a few:

Gabrielle Douglas (Virginia Beach) Gymnast. Olympic Gold Medalist.

Allen Iverson (Hampton) Basketball. Rookie of the Year. League MVP. Naismith Memorial Basketball Hall of Fame.

Bruce Smith (Williamsburg) Football. 2-time Super Bowl Champion. Pro Football Hall of Fame.

Gabby Douglas. *(Agência Brasil Fotografias / Creative Commons)*

Sam Snead (Hot Springs) Golf. 3 Masters Wins. 3 PGA Titles.

Justin Verlander *(Keith Allison/ Creative Commons, cropped)*

Justin Verlander (Manakin-Sabot) Baseball. Rookie of the Year. League MVP. Cy Young winner.

Pernell "Sweet Pea" Whitaker (Norfolk) Boxing. Welterweight and Lightweight Champion. International Boxing Hall of Fame.

Patsy Cline
We Finally Made It

In addition to the great Bill "Bojangles" Robinson, Virginia produced another award-winning tap dancer. In 1936, four-year-old Virginia Patterson Hensley won a local talent contest with her tap-dancing skills. Few people remember that contest, the name Virginia Hensley, or her tap dancing. It was in another contest, under another name, and with another talent that she became famous.

She was born in Winchester, in the northern tip of Virginia in 1932. Her mother, Hilda, was only 16 years old when Virginia was born. They were so close in age that her mother would later say they were more like sisters than mother and daughter. They were certainly partners in her success.

Times were especially tough during the 1930's. There were few job opportunities and most families had little money. One of the bright spots for many Americans was a visit to the local movie house. Virginia, or Ginny as she was called, especially loved seeing

PATSY CLINE

COUNTRY & WESTERN SINGER, 1932-1963

29 USA

Patsy Cline was honored by the U.S. Postal service with this stamp.

Shirley Temple movies. After watching one of Shirley's films, Ginny tap danced down the street, all the way home.

At the age of 13, she had a near-death experience when she contracted *rheumatic fever*. She was placed under an oxygen tent to help her breathing. She would later say that when she recovered, she discovered she had a huge and powerful singing voice like Kate Smith, another Virginia-born artist famous for singing the song "God Bless America."

Soon, Ginny was singing at church, in talent contests, and on local radio. Her mother was involved in all of these efforts. As a seamstress, Hilda made her stage costumes using a foot-powered sewing machine. Hilda used what little money the family had to purchase an upright piano that Ginny taught herself to play.

By the time Ginny was 16, the family had moved around the state 19 times before settling into a small rented Winchester home on South Kent Street. Her father was no longer around, leaving Ginny and Hilda to fend for themselves. To help make ends meet, Ginny dropped out of school to scoop ice cream at the local drug store. All the while, she and her mother continued to pursue her dream of a music career.

Small success slowly built one after another. She appeared in touring country music shows and got a recording contract with Four Star Records.

The Four Star contract paid her very little money and restricted which songs she could sing. Fortunately, one of the songs was a number called "Walkin' After Midnight." Her television performance of this song would change her life.

During the 1950's there were few entertainers more successful

Promotional photo. *(Public Domain)*

and powerful than Arthur Godfrey. He had radio shows throughout the week, a morning television show Monday through Friday, and two evening shows. One of those evening shows was "Arthur Godfrey's Talent Scouts." Long before "American Idol" and other televised contests, "Talent Scouts" introduced up and coming performers to the nation. The winner was chosen by the cheers of the audience measured by a machine called the "Applause Meter." The performer receiving the loudest applause was the winner.

In order to compete on "Talent Scouts," contestants had to have a talent agent who would introduce them. The rules stated that the talent agent could not be a relative. By now, Ginny was performing under the stage name "Patsy Cline." Her mother appeared as her talent agent and didn't let on that they were related.

After an introduction, Patsy sang. The audience cheered. The "Applause Meter" was pushed to its limits. And a star was born.

"Walkin' After Midnight" was released as a single, and became a country hit nationwide. Even more impressive, and unusual for the time, it "crossed over" to the popular charts and became a hit with non-country music fans.

Teaming up with legendary music producer Owen Bradley, she produced hit after hit including the song "Crazy" written by Willie Nelson. She was made a member of the *Grand Ole Opry*. With money she earned, she was able to buy that home on South Kent Street for her mother.

Since her passing in 1963, her fame has only increased. Her greatest hits album has sold over 10 million copies.

The Patsy Cline Historic Home in Winchester. *(Author)*

She became the first woman inducted into the Country Music Hall of Fame. She continues to appear on lists as one of the top female singers of all time.

Her Winchester home is now a

museum that is open to the public. Inside, you can see a foot-powered sewing machine like the one Hilda used to make little Ginny's first costumes, you can see an upright piano like the one her mother bought her, and on top of that piano is a picture of Patsy. On it, Patsy has written a note to her biggest supporter, "To Mom: We Finally Made It. All My Love. Patsy Cline."

(Author)

A Friend and Mentor...

Loretta Lynn receiving the Presidential Medal of Freedom from Barack Obama. *(Rena Schild / Shutterstock)*

Patsy Cline's early life taught her survival skills that she used in her career and her personal life. She became a friend and mentor to several women who would also become music legends. Loretta (*Coal Miner's Daughter*) Lynn and Brenda (*Rockin' Around the Christmas Tree*) Lee received help and learned how to thrive in a tough business through Patsy's friendship.

Current singers like Carrie Underwood continue to acknowledge and pay tribute to her great talent.

(Photo Illustration: Public Domain, Brian Friedman/Shutterstock)

Booker T. Washington
The Other Washington

It's the early 1860's and a young boy named Booker is helping the little girl who lives in the farmhouse carry her books to school. Helping others gain an education is something Booker will spend most of his life doing. On this day, he can only walk up to the door of the school and no further. He peers into the classroom, filled with books, and a blackboard with chalk images, and then the door closes in his face. He is not allowed into the classroom. At this time in Virginia, it was against the law to teach enslaved, black people to read.

Still, Booker held on to the image of that classroom. He later said, ***"The picture of several dozen boys and girls in a schoolroom engaged in study made a deep impression upon me, and I had the feeling that to get into a schoolhouse and study in this way would be about the same as getting into paradise."***

He was born on April 5, 1856 on a farm in Franklin County, in western Virginia, he was given the name Booker. The last name, Washington, would be added later. Like many others across the South, his ancestors had been kidnapped from Africa and elsewhere, then brought here to work for no pay and with no rights. He lived in a small shack on the farm, sleeping on top of rags. He never sat down for a meal with his family. He never knew his father. He didn't know he was a

Booker T. Washington's birthplace is now a National Monument. There, you can see a re-creation of his first home. *(Author)*

slave until one night he heard his mother praying that one day, slavery would end and her family would be free.

Her prayers would soon be answered. The *Emancipation Proclamation*, written by Abraham Lincoln, offered hope for freedom but it took the North winning the Civil War to fulfill that promise.

Booker and his family could now join their step-father in West Virginia. Booker and his brothers joined

The exterior of Booker T. Washington's birthplace.
(Author)

him working in the coal mines. It was hard and dangerous work. Booker had not given up on his dream of an education and when a school for black children opened, he was able to attend when he was not at work. It was at work in the mines that he heard of a place called the Hampton Normal and Agricultural Institute where he could further his studies.

He gathered what little money he had and headed for Hampton, Virginia. He wasn't sure how far away it was or if they would even accept him, but he headed off just the same. If fact, it was a 500-mile journey. He took a stagecoach as his money would allow, hitchhiked, and walked until he found his way to Hampton.

When he arrived, he looked like someone who had

hitchhiked and walked over 500 miles. Still, his *resourcefulness* and dedication to an education must have impressed them for he was allowed to attend the school. He was given a job as a janitor to help pay for his education.

A bust of Booker T. Washington at the National Monument. *(Author)*

Life on campus was an eye-opening experience for Booker. He had never slept on a bed before and the first night, he lay underneath both sets of the sheets. Soon, he discovered what to do.

Hampton offered classes in math and writing. It also taught biology and had a working farm where students worked and learned successful farming methods. Booker graduated with honors at the age of 19.

Booker understood the importance of education to life success and returned home where he taught others. His time back at home was short-lived. Hampton asked him to return to the school where he would become a teacher to Native Americans. He was also able to continue his own education.

His skill as a teacher and public speaker, combined with his willingness to work hard, had caught the attention of Hampton Institute's leader, General Samuel Chapman Armstrong. When the state of Alabama searched for a leader of a new school for black teachers and students, Armstrong recommended Booker.

He arrived in Tuskegee, Alabama, to find an empty field. There were no buildings, no teachers, and no

Puppeteers Wesley Huff and Josh Messick review the Emancipation Proclamation with Abraham Lincoln. *(Author)*

students. As he had throughout his life, he looked past the obstacles and was soon teaching in a borrowed room in a nearby church. With fundraising efforts, he was able to buy more property to create a

The Tuskegee Institute campus. *(Public domain)*

farm which would help teach skills to the students and provide food and income.

When it was time to create their own buildings, Booker decided that the students would cut and prepare the lumber and create the bricks for the buildings. Brickmaking proved to be the task that would not come easily to Booker. He and the students tried three times to build a kiln oven to bake mud and clay into bricks. Three times they failed. With no more money, Booker *pawned* his watch in order to get enough money for a fourth try. This time, the kiln worked and bricks were properly baked. Finally, Tuskegee had classrooms built by the students with bricks they had made with their own hands. Soon, people of all colors were coming to Tuskegee to buy their bricks.

The Tuskegee Normal School became known throughout the country. That's not to say Booker T. Washington and his techniques were not without critics. Some parents did not want their children working with pigs and stomping around in mud, making bricks. Booker felt that physical work was an important life skill. Others thought that Booker T. Washington moved too slowly in seeking equal rights for African Americans. Despite the nay-sayers, the success of Booker T. Washington's

Booker T. Washington portrait. The "T." is for "Taliaferro," which his mother gave him. He gave himself the last name "Washington" when he entered school. *(Public domain)*

The Emancipation Oak in Hampton, Virginia. This is the spot where the Emancipation Proclamation was first read in the South. It was also the location where another Virginian, Mary Peake, taught reading to newly-freed children. *(Author)*

approach cannot be ignored.

Today, a statue of Booker T. Washington stands on the grounds of Hampton University. He points across the street to the Emancipation Oak. This tree was standing during the Civil War and was the very place that Lincoln's Emancipation Proclamation was first read in the South. Booker was born at a time when he and his family were denied the opportunity to read and write. There was only the promise of future freedom. In Booker's lifetime, that promise was fulfilled. Through hard work, he was able to get an education and then build a school that continues to touch lives and change our world.

Booker T. Washington statue on the campus of Hampton
University. *(Author)*

Final Thoughts...

If you've seen one of our shows, you know that I often come onstage at the end and ask, "What did we learn today?" From this group of amazing people, we can learn so much.

Booker T. Washington was not content to just get an education, he wanted to share the power of knowledge with others. He gave people the ability to find a rewarding career and a rewarding life.

Bill Robinson's dancing skill allowed him to gain great wealth which he was happy to share with others. If he saw a hungry family or someone without a home or someone in danger, he used his wealth to make their lives better. Likewise, Arthur Ashe used his fame from tennis to make a difference in the way people treat one another.

George Washington would have been happiest working on his farm. Time and again, he answered duty's call and as a result, the United States was born. While not perfect, our system of elected government gives Americans the power to make this country better today than it was yesterday.

Sunset in the Shenandoah National Park. (christianthiel.net / Shutterstock)

Like others in this book, Patsy Cline and Ella Fitzgerald had difficult childhoods. Despite their challenges, they rose to the top.

Pocahontas never forgot the riches found in Virginia. Her lessons are still important today. Virginia is a beautiful place to live. Its richness is enhanced by the diverse and talented people who live there.

How will you use your talents to help others?

Bibliography

Biography. *Bill Bojangles Robinson.* Mimi Washington writer, Torrie Rosenzweig director, 1997.

Buckley Jr., James. *Who Was Booker T. Washington?* New York, Penguin Workshop, 2018.

Chernow, Ron. *Washington: A Life*. New York, Penguin Books, 2011.

Edwards, Roberta. *Who Was George Washington?* New York, Penguin Workshop, 2009.

Ella Fitzgerald: Just One of Those Things. Leslie Woodhead director. 2019.

Fritz, Jean. *The Double Life of Pocahontas.* London, Puffin Books, 2002.

Hankins, James and Mitgang, N. R. *Mr. Bojangles: the biography of Bill Robinson*. New York, William Morrow and Company, Inc., 1988.

Hubbard, Crystal. *The Story of Tennis Champion Arthur Ashe.* New York, Lee & Low Books, 2018.

Lynn, Loretta. *Me and Patsy Kickin' Up Dust*. New York, Grand Central Publishing, 2021.

Remembering Patsy. Mark Hall writer-director, Hallway Music Holdings, 1993.

Unger, Harlow Giles. *"Mr. President" George Washington and the Making of the Nation's Highest Office.* Boston, Da Capo Press, 2013.

Washington, Booker T. *Up From Slavery.* Chapel Hill, Gutenberg digital reprint, 2008.

Thanks to

Christine Almassy, Interpretive Park Guide, George Washington Birthplace National Monument, Colonial Beach, VA.

Michelle Gilliam, Ella Fitzgerald Theater, Downing-Gross Cultural Arts Center, Newport News, VA.

Karen Helm and Hannah McDonald, Patsy Cline Historic House, Winchester, VA.

Powhatan Red Cloud-Owen, Chickahominy Tribe. (2007 interviews)

Beth Richardson, The Pocahontas Museum, Gloucester, VA.

Timothy Sims, Chief of Interpretation, Booker T. Washington National Monument, Hardy, VA.

Jesse Parker, Virginia Musical Museum, Williamsburg, VA.

Jordan Petty, George Washington's Mount Vernon, Alexandria, VA.

Karenne Wood, Monacan Tribe. (2007 interviews)

The trademarks mentioned in this book are for editorial purposes only and do not imply endorsement by or for the related companies.

"Bojangles'" is a trademark of Bojangles OPCO, LLC

"Grammy Award" is a trademark of the National Academy of Recording Arts & Sciences, Inc.

"Tony Award ®" is a trademark of the American Theatre Wing, Inc.

Glossary

Ambassador – A person who represents one group or country to another group or country.

Britain / British – A large island in Europe which includes England, Scotland, and Wales. All are part of the United Kingdom.

Colony / Colonist – A group that is governed by a foreign or distant country.

Emancipation Proclamation - President Abraham Lincoln's order which freed enslaved people in the southern states. Its effect was not immediate for most until the end of the Civil War.

Exaggerated – Making something sound bigger or better or worse than it really is.

Grammy Award – Awards given by the Recording Academy.

Grand Ole Opry – Since 1925, a weekly radio program presenting county music. It is a great industry honor to be a performing member of the Opry.

Paramount Chief – The top leader of a group or organization. Powhatan was the *Paramount Chief* over many other chiefs.

Pawn – Something given in value for a loan of money.

Resourcefulness – Using any available method to solve a problem.

Rheumatic fever – A disease of the heart and joints that can develop after a strep throat infection.

Scat – Wordless singing that blends in with other instruments in a song.

Tony Award – Awards given by the American Theater Wing for excellence on Broadway and regional theaters.

David Messick is the founder of Rainbow Puppet Productions. He has written several children's books and dozens of original children's musicals that have been performed at the Smithsonian, New York's American Museum of Natural History, and many other organizations. He has also worked on development projects for the Oprah Winfrey Show and the Disney Channel and worked with many legendary performers. He and his wife Marcy were blessed with two boys... Joshua and Luke.
http://davidmessick.com

Liu Light is an illustrator and multimedia designer in California. Light has illustrated a number of children's books with a focus on books featuring diverse voices and stories for such organizations as Shout Mouse Press and Rainbow Puppet Productions. Liu also enjoys drawing animations and comics.
http://liulight.com

Other books from David and Liu:
The Amazing Adventures of Chessie the Manatee
Creatures Great and Small
Mary Peake and the Mighty Acorn
The Mother Goose Show
Never Give Up, Short Stories about Big Dreams
Open a Book
The Precarious Predicaments of Pinocchio
The Tall, the Tough, and the Tiny
You Can Do That? Amazing People with Amazing Jobs

Audio Programs from David and the Rainbow Puppets:
The Amazing Adventures of Chessie the Manatee
From the Sea to the Sky
Jonah
The Mother Goose Travelling Rock and Roll Show
A Pirate Party
The Really Big Dinosaur Show
Toyland!
The Wetland Revue
The Wright Brothers— See Us Fly!
Available at Amazon.com, RainbowPuppets.com, and DavidMessick.com